# Parenting for Academic Success

## A Curriculum for Families Learning English

# Unit 12:

# Celebrate Family Learning

## PARENT WORKBOOK

### Lesson 1: Rejoice in Accomplishments

*National Center for Family Literacy*

DELTA PUBLISHING COMPANY
A Divison of DELTA SYSTEMS CO., INC.
1400 Miller Parkway
McHenry, IL 60050 USA
(800) 323-8270 or (815) 363-3582
www.delta-systems.com

Printed in the United States of America

Parent Workbook 12 ISBN-10: 1-932748-40-7
ISBN-13: 978-1-932748-40-6

## Acknowledgments

*Parenting for Academic Success: A Curriculum for Families Learning English* was developed by the National Center for Family Literacy (NCFL) in collaboration with the Center for Applied Linguistics (CAL) and K. Lynn Savage, English as a Second Language (ESL) Teacher and Training Consultant.

Principle Curriculum Authors: Janet M. Fulton (NCFL), Laura Golden (CAL), Dr. Betty Ansin Smallwood (CAL), and K. Lynn Savage, Educational Consultant.

Special thanks to the Toyota Family Literacy Program, which piloted these materials in Washington, DC; New York, NY: Providence, RI; Chicago, IL; and Los Angeles, CA.

The Verizon Foundation provided original funding for the development of this curriculum and supports the National Center for Family Literacy in its development of resources for English language learners. Verizon's support of the literacy cause includes Thinkfinity.org, a free digital learning platform that advances learning in traditional settings and beyond the classroom. Visit the Thinkfinity Literacy Network managed by the National Center for Family Literacy and ProLiteracy Worldwide on Thinkfinity.org for free online courses and resources that support literacy across the life span.

Special thanks to Jennifer McMaster (NCFL) for her editing expertise.

## A Message for Parents

This program is designed for parents who want to build their English language skills. The program also will help you learn ways to help your child improve his or her skills to succeed in school.

You will do activities to learn and practice reading, writing, speaking and listening in English. These activities also share information about how children learn to speak and read English. Each lesson has an activity you can do with your child at home.

When you support your child's learning at home, your child learns how language works.

Doing family learning activities together:

- Helps you be your child's first teacher.
- Helps you learn how your child learns.
- Makes learning fun.
- Supports your child's learning outside the classroom.

You can help your child learn every day. This program will help you help your child to learn.

## Un Mensaje para Padres

Este programa está creado para padres que quieren mejorar sus destrezas en inglés. A la misma vez el programa les va a ayudar apoyar el aprendizaje de sus niños y a prepararlos para tener éxito escolar cuando entran a las escuelas.

Dentro encontrarán actividades para que mejoren sus destrezas de lectura, escritura, y conversación en inglés. Las actividades van a compartir información acerca de cómo aprenden los niños a hablar y leer en inglés. Cada lección tiene actividades para hacer en casa con sus niños.

Cuando usted apoya el aprendizaje de su niño en casa, él o ella aprende como se usa el lenguaje.

Cuando hacen actividades escolares juntos:

- Le ayuda ser el primer maestro de su niño.
- Le ayuda aprender como aprende su niño.
- Aprendiendo conceptos es más divertido.
- Apoya el aprendizaje de su niño fuera del salón de clase.

Le puede ayudar a su niño diariamente. Este programa le ayuda apoyar el aprendizaje de su niño.

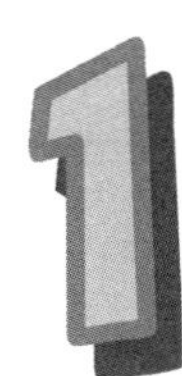

# LESSON 1: Rejoice in Accomplishments

## Lesson Goal
Summarize learning and celebrate program accomplishments.

## Lesson Objectives
Today we will:

- Read a poem.
- Write a poem.
- Summarize learning.
- Role play.
- Celebrate!

## Lesson Warm–Up
1. Think about something you liked about this program.

   **Example:** *I liked it when Maria told us that she took part in her first parent–teacher meeting and that it went well.*

   I liked ____________________________________________

   ____________________________________________

   ____________________________________________.

2. Share what you liked about the program with your classmates.

## Points to Remember

Help strengthen the skills your child needs to be successful in school. It will:

- Improve your own language and literacy skills.
- Develop your child's language and literacy skills (in English and your home language).
- Help your child learn to read and write (in English and your home language).
- Help you and your child learn about the U.S. school system.

Can you add some more important points to this list?

______________________________________________

______________________________________________

______________________________________________

______________________________________________

## Activity 1: Key Vocabulary

Words in this lesson are listed below. Use the Key Vocabulary pages to build your vocabulary.

1. Review the words. Which ones do you know?

| Word Part | Word | Example | Translation |
|---|---|---|---|
| adjective | drowsy | | |
| adjective | funny | | |
| adjective | happy | | |
| adjective | loving | | |
| adjective | precious | | |
| adjective | snuggly | | |
| verb | accomplish | | |
| verb | appreciate | | |
| verb | celebrate | | |
| | | | |
| | | | |
| | | | |
| | | | |
| | | | |
| | | | |
| | | | |
| | | | |

2. Practice using Key Vocabulary words. Mark the parts of speech for each word pair below.

**Example:** *sing – singer*
*verb noun*

**Example:** *quick – quickly*
*adjective adverb*

- celebrate – celebration
- appreciate – appreciation
- accomplish – accomplishment
- translate – translation
- care – careful
- love – lovely
- snuggle – snuggly
- fun – funny
- happy – happiness

3. Practice using Key Vocabulary words. Write two sentences with two Key Vocabulary words.

**Example:** *I get drowsy in the afternoon.*

______________________________________________

______________________________________________.

______________________________________________

______________________________________________.

## Activity 2: Reading to the Children

1. Listen as your teacher reads this poem.

**"Reading to the Children"**

Open books and open faces,
Loving time and loving places.

Loving words and loving looks,
Precious voices, precious books.

Open books for open eyes,
Snuggly stories, snug and wise.

Funny figures, funny rhymes,
Sunny pictures, sunny times.

Minds so drowsy, minds awake,
Hearts that give and hearts that take.

Questions new and questions old,
Answers silver, answers gold.

Pictures touched and pages turned,
Lessons offered, lessons learned.

Happy smiles and happy laughter,
Happy memories ever after.

*by Kathryn Lindskoog and Ranelda Hunsicker*



2. Read the poem with a partner.

3. Answer these questions.

▸ What is the poem about?

The poem is about ______________________________________________

__________________________________________________________________

__________________________________________________________________.

▸ Why is it important to read to children?

It is important to read to children because: _______________________

__________________________________________________________________.

4. Read these definitions.

**Adjectives:** Words that describe or tell something about nouns or pronouns.

**Nouns:** Words used to name people, places and things.

5. List some adjectives used in the poem. List the words they describe.

| Adjectives | Nouns Described |
|---|---|
| **Example:** *open* | **Example:** *books, faces* |
| | |
| | |
| | |
| | |
| | |
| | |
| | |

## Activity 3: Write a "First Letter Poem"

1. Read the definition for a "first–letter poem."

| A **first–letter poem** is a poem written using the letters of a word. |
|---|

2. Write a "first–letter poem." Express thoughts about the word *writing*.
   - For each letter, write a word or words that start with that letter.
   - Give your poem a title.

| **Title:** | |
|---|---|
| **W** | |
| **R** | |
| **I** | |
| **T** | |
| **I** | |
| **N** | |
| **G** | |
| **By:** | |

3. Share your "first–letter poem" with the class.

4. Read these "first–letter poem" examples.

| **Title: Writing** | |
|---|---|
| **W** | **W**riting is |
| **R** | **R**eading and writing |
| **I** | **I**ntegrated |
| **T** | **T**ogether |
| **I** | **I**n |
| **N** | **N**otes and narratives |
| **G** | **G**ood and sometimes not so good, I try.<br>**G**ood bye! |
| **By:** Betty Ansin Smallwood, 2000 | |

| **Title: People** | |
|---|---|
| **P** | **P**lease people |
| **E** | **E**verywhere and everyone |
| **O** | **O**n this our one and only |
| **P** | **P**lanet |
| **L** | **L**et's try to love and understand |
| **E** | **E**ach other. |
| **By:** Betty Ansin Smallwood, 1994 | |

5. With a partner, write a "first–letter poem" using the word *reading*.

| **Title:** | |
|---|---|
| **R** | |
| **E** | |
| **A** | |
| **D** | |
| **I** | |
| **N** | |
| **G** | |
| **By:** | |

6. Share your "first–letter poem" with the class.

7. Write a "first–letter poem." Select your own word.

| Title: | |
|---|---|
| | |
| | |
| | |
| | |
| | |
| | |
| | |
| | |
| | |
| | |
| By: | |

## Activity 4: What We Have Learned

1. Finish each sentence about your experience in this program.

   As a result of this program,

   I feel ______________________________________________
   ______________________________________________
   ______________________________________________.

   I like ______________________________________________
   ______________________________________________
   ______________________________________________.

   I learned ______________________________________________
   ______________________________________________
   ______________________________________________.

   I believe ______________________________________________
   ______________________________________________
   ______________________________________________.

   I plan to ______________________________________________
   ______________________________________________
   ______________________________________ with my child.

   I plan to ______________________________________________
   ______________________________________________
   ______________________________________ for myself.

   I want to learn more about ______________________________
   ______________________________________________
   ______________________________________________.

2. Share your sentences with the class.

3. I also want to say ______________________________________________
______________________________________________________________
______________________________________________________________.

4. Review the goals you set for yourself in your *Parent Workbook*, Unit 1: Plan for Success.

   - What were your goals for this program?
   ______________________________________________________________
   ______________________________________________________________
   ______________________________________________________________.

   - How have you met your goals for this program?
   ______________________________________________________________
   ______________________________________________________________
   ______________________________________________________________.

   - What are your goals for reading and writing with your child?
   ______________________________________________________________
   ______________________________________________________________
   ______________________________________________________________.

5. Reflect on some important ideas and vocabulary words you heard in this lesson.
   - Read the words below.
   - With the class, talk about these words.
   - Add any new words you want to remember below.

- celebrate
- celebration
- accomplish
- accomplishment
- 
- 
- 

6. Review the ideas in the lesson.

   **Lesson 1: Rejoice in Accomplishments**
   Today we looked back. We talked about what we remembered and what was fun about this program. We read a poem about reading to children. We talked about the goals we set and how we met them. We also set some goals for reading and writing with our child.

7. Do you have any other important ideas you learned from this lesson?
   - List them below.
   - Share your ideas with the class.

   ________________________________________

   ________________________________________

   ________________________________________

   ________________________________________

## Activity 5: Role Play With Friends

1. Role play this situation with a partner.
    - Your friend's child is starting kindergarten this fall.
    - What could your friend do to help his or her child build the skills needed to be successful in school?
    - Take turns with your partner to play each part.
2. Share your role play with the class.

## Parent Survey

This survey is to evaluate the unit on **Celebrate Family Learning**. There are no wrong answers and you will not be asked to talk about your answers.

1. What information did you learn from the Celebrate Family Learning unit?

_______________________________________________

_______________________________________________

_______________________________________________

2. What else would you like to know about the Celebrate Family Learning unit?

_______________________________________________

_______________________________________________

_______________________________________________

3. How will the information help you help your child?

_______________________________________________

_______________________________________________

_______________________________________________

4. Check (✔) one of the following statements about this unit.

__________ I understood everything.

__________ I understood most of it.

__________ I understood some of it.

__________ I understood a little of it.

__________ I did not understand any of it.

**When you have finished this survey, please give it to your teacher.**

## Encuesta a los padres

Esta encuesta es para evaluar la unidad de **Celebrando el aprendizaje de la Familia**. No existen respuestas incorrectas y no se le pedirá que comente lo que respondió.

1. ¿Qué cosas aprendió en la unidad de Celebrando el aprendizaje de la Familia?

______________________________________________

______________________________________________

______________________________________________

2. ¿Qué otras cosas le gustarían saber acerca de la unidad de Celebrando el aprendizaje de la Familia?

______________________________________________

______________________________________________

______________________________________________

3. ¿De qué manera le ayudará a usted esta información para poder ayudar a su niño?

______________________________________________

______________________________________________

______________________________________________

4. Marque (✔) sólo una de las siguientes afirmaciones sobre esta unidad.

__________ Entendí todo.

__________ Entendí la mayoría de las cosas.

__________ Entendí algunas cosas.

__________ Entendí un poco.

__________ No entendí en absoluto.

**Cuando haya finalizado esta encuesta, entréguesela a su maestro.**